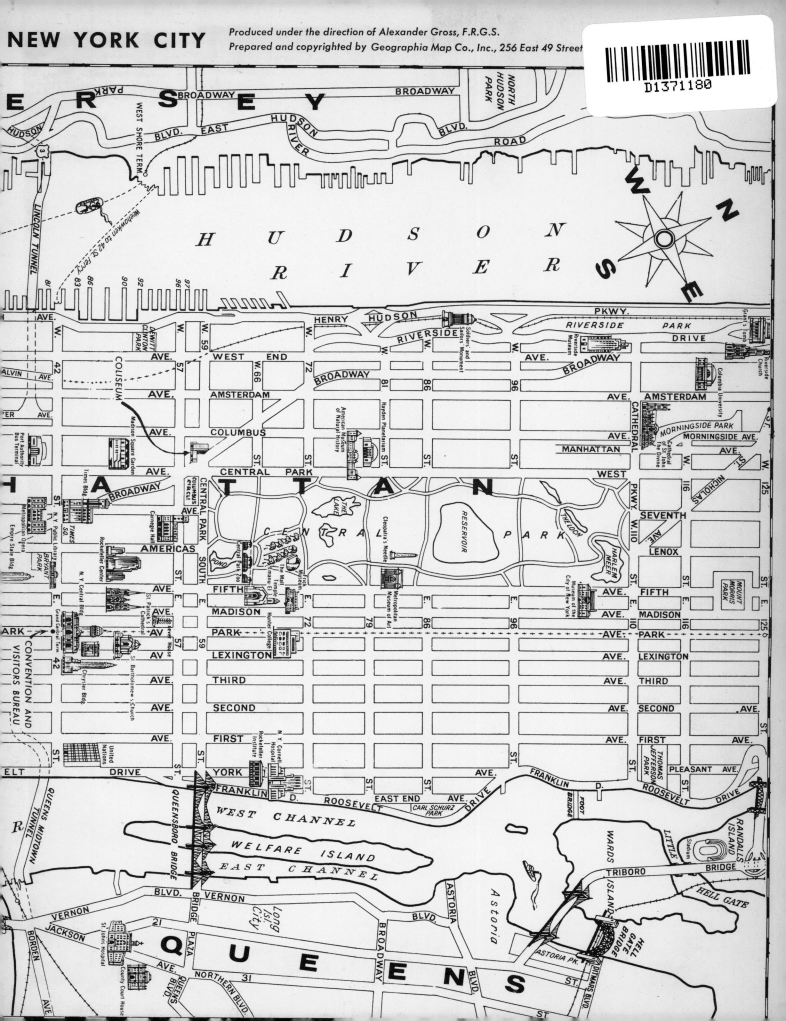

NEW YORK CITY

Produced under the direction of Alexander Gross, F.R.G.S.
Prepared and copyrighted by Geographia Map Co., Inc., 256 East 49 Street

D1371180

THE STATUE OF LIBERTY, America's most famous symbol and landmark, welcomes all who come through New York Harbor. Officially called "Liberty Enlightening the World," the statue, designed by Frederic Auguste Bartholdi, was presented by the French people to the United States on July 4, 1884, in commemoration of our Independence Day in 1776.

It is the world's largest statue. The torch can hold a dozen people; the head is ten feet wide and seventeen feet high; the right index finger is eight feet long and five feet around. The skyline and harbor view from the observatory, just under the crown, is spectacular.

Give me your tired, your poor,
Your huddled masses yearning to breathe free,
The wretched refuse of your teeming shore,
Send these, the homeless, tempest-tossed, to me:
I lift my lamp beside the golden door.

Inscription for the Statue of Liberty
—EMMA LAZARUS (1849-1887)

NEW YORK
IN PHOTOGRAPHS

Edited by William Cole and Julia Colmore

SIMON AND SCHUSTER · NEW YORK · 1961

FIRST PRINTING

LIBRARY OF CONGRESS CATALOG CARD NUMBER: 61-15118

PRINTED BY THE MURRAY PRINTING CO., FORGE VILLAGE, MASS.; BOUND BY H. WOLFF BOOK MFG. CO., NEW YORK

MANHATTAN ISLAND is twelve and a half miles long and only two and a half miles wide at its broadest point. Although fewer than two million of the city's eight million people live on the island, it is in essence what the world regards as "New York City." Here is the heart of America's business and culture; here is the awesome city of skyscrapers, host to more than twenty million visitors each year.

LOOKING NORTH FROM THE HARBOR, you see the cluster of tall buildings in the financial district—the world's most famous skyline. At last count, there were 84 skyscrapers over thirty stories high in Manhattan. (New York's centerpiece, the Empire State Building—at top of photograph—is 102 stories.) But last counts are always out of date in changing Manhattan. New skyscrapers seem to spring up overnight, and twenty or thirty are at this moment either just completed or in construction.

5

SOUTH OF CENTRAL PARK is the busy midtown area: Times Square, Rockefeller Center, the shopping districts and the United Nations. To the right are the Hudson River and New Jersey; on the left are the East River, Queens and Brooklyn. At the tip of the island is the financial district. Beyond it is The Narrows, between Brooklyn and Staten Island, through which ships from all over the world enter New York Harbor.

It is an easy city to find your way around; the avenues run straight down the island (with the exception of Broadway, which swerves down diagonally), and most of the cross streets are logically numbered.

6

A TOURIST'S-EYE VIEW of lower Manhattan from the sight-seeing boats that circle the island.

8

9

THE EMPIRE STATE BUILDING, on Fifth Avenue from 33 to 34 Streets, is the tallest building in the world. It rises 1,472 feet — about a quarter of a mile — above Manhattan. Atop its 102 stories is a 22-story television tower that services all of the city's seven TV stations. The beacons at the 90th-floor level are the world's most powerful; they may be seen from the air 300 miles away and serve as an inland lighthouse for ships at sea and approaching planes. From the observatories (on the 86th and 102nd floors) visitors can see 50 miles away into five states on a clear day. About a million people visit these observatories each year; nearly 1,000 people are employed the year round in maintenance and operation; there are 25,000 occupants.

LOOKING NORTH AT MIDTOWN MANHATTAN from the observatory of the Empire State Building. On the left, Central Park and Rockefeller Center; on the right, Manhattan's second-tallest skyscraper, the 77-story Chrysler Building; and at the far right, the United Nations.

Nighttime view from the 87th floor of the Empire State Building showing why Broadway, at Times Square, is called "The Great White Way." Thousands upon thousands of multicolored light bulbs in immense advertising displays and on theater and movie marquees make this the brightest ten blocks in the world. There is a greater concentration of restaurants, night clubs, theaters, signs, and people here than anywhere else. Shabby by day, jazzy by night, it is the "Crossroads of the World," and certainly at least half the people on the Square at any moment are out-of-town visitors.

THE SUBWAY SYSTEM is efficient and fast, but, particularly at busy stations like Times Square, should be shunned during rush hours by anyone with either a delicate constitution or a respect for his fellow man.

42 STREET, between Seventh and Eighth Avenues, is a succession of "grind" movie houses showing continuous double features from early morning until late at night. On the rest of the block are cut-rate book and record stores, a flea circus, cafeterias, and bars.

TIMES
SQUARE

THE WORLD'S LARGEST NEW YEAR'S EVE PARTY is a tradition in Times Square, where thousands of people gather to watch the clock on the Times Tower herald another year.

In the display windows of the pizza parlors the making of the pies is a show in itself.

16

THEATER INTERMISSION time during the warm months brings patrons out to the street.

TWO KINDS OF SIGHT-SEEING TOURS [RIGHT] are available for visitors. Bus tours generally cover the high spots: Times Square, Harlem, Fifth Avenue, Wall Street and Chinatown. Excursion boats circle Manhattan and venture out into the harbor for a close-up of the Statue of Liberty.

At the foot of the Times Tower is the Out of Town Newspaper stand, featuring publications — few more than a day old — from every major city in the United States. In the subway entrance under the same building there is a shop specializing in foreign newspapers and periodicals.

18

17

NEW YORK'S PIGEONS — Just as the eagle is the American bird, the pigeon is New York City's. Here a bird lover makes her daily contribution to their welfare. There are an estimated 200,000 pigeons in the city.

19

20

LINDY'S, Broadway and 51 Street [LEFT] — Broadway celebrities such as entertainers Milton Berle and Phil Silvers, columnists Walter Winchell and Leonard Lyons, and frequenters of Tin Pan Alley (pop singer Connie Francis, shown here) frequent Lindy's Restaurant (lightly disguised as "Mindy's" in Damon Runyon's stories about Broadway characters).

INFORMATION CENTER, Times Square [RIGHT] — This is the where-to-go and how-to-get-there center for visitors to New York.

THE PALLADIUM, Broadway between 53 and 54 Streets [RIGHT] — Known variously as the "Cha Cha Citadel" or the "Mambo Mecca," this huge dance hall is where all the popular Latin American dances get their start. There might be anywhere from two to six orchestras alternating on an evening. Wednesday is "Celebrity Night," when there is both an amateur contest and a professional exhibition.

LATIN QUARTER, Broadway and 48 Street [LEFT] — Broadway's biggest night club entertains as many as a thousand people a night. The elaborate show brings on lovely girls (with and without costumes) and stars such as Sophie Tucker, Frankie Laine and Milton Berle.

ROCKEFELLER CENTER

THIS CITY WITHIN A CITY, extending from 48 to 52 Streets, Fifth Avenue to Avenue of the Americas, is a complex of sixteen buildings, the newest of which is the Time & Life Building (upper right). The 70-story RCA Building, sometimes called "Radio City," is the tallest. All the buildings connect underground, where there are shopping arcades and restaurants. The total daytime population of Rockefeller Center is 175,000.

TIME & LIFE BUILDING — Opened in 1959, the 48-story Time & Life Building is on Avenue of the Americas between 50 and 51 Streets.

ATLAS, Fifth Avenue between 50 and 51 Streets — The most photographed object in the city is the 45-foot Atlas in front of the International Building. At almost any hour of the day one or more "photobugs" can be seen crouching down before it getting angle shots, such as this one.

OUTDOOR SKATING POND [BELOW, RIGHT] — Some of the world's finest figure skaters do their practicing here. In the summer months the rink is converted to an outdoor restaurant.

CHRISTMAS DISPLAY [BELOW] — A giant tree (this one is 64 feet high) and an elaborate display in the Channel Gardens are an annual specialty. The façade of Saks Fifth Avenue in the background ties in with the spirit.

RADIO CITY MUSIC HALL — Eight million people come each year to the world's largest theater. It has a seating capacity of 6,200 and a stage a city block long. First-run movies and lavish productions featuring the Corps de Ballet and the Music Hall Rockettes — thirty-six girls who dance with clockwork precision — keep the theater filled to capacity, especially during the holiday season.

INSIDE THE TV STUDIOS — One of the musts for any tourist in New York is a visit to a major television show. Tickets must be written for far in advance. Here is how the in-person visitor sees the Jack Paar Show.

30

31

LA FONDA DEL SOL, in the Time & Life Building, specializing in the cuisines of South America, Central America and Mexico, is the most colorful new restaurant in the city. In this "Inn of the Sun," sun symbols are everywhere and the décor is brilliant with native arts and crafts. The rotisserie wall is emblazoned with the names of traditional drinks and dishes, creating a posterlike effect.

32

33

CAFE LOUIS XIV, off Fifth Avenue on 49 Street, is a handsome and graceful restaurant with a patrician air. Thick carpets, red plush seats and tall windows give it an atmosphere of hushed luxury.

ST. PATRICK'S CATHEDRAL, Fifth Avenue, 50 to 51 Streets — The Cathedral of the Roman Catholic Archdiocese of New York. The design of this impressive Gothic structure is based on the Cathedral of Cologne. St. Patrick's was over thirty years in construction. The bronze doors and the rose windows over the entrance are particularly impressive.

THE EASTER PARADE [BELOW, LEFT]—Spring finery blossoms, and in front of St. Patrick's the Avenue is jammed with strollers, photographers and pretty girls in flowered hats.

OLIVETTI, 584 Fifth Avenue [BELOW, RIGHT]—The lure of something for nothing — even if it's only the opportunity to type "the quick brown fox . . ." — stops hundreds of passers-by every day at the portable typewriter set up outside the handsome Olivetti showroom.

34

35

FIFTH AVENUE

FIFTH AVENUE is to New York what the Champs-Elysées is to Paris and what Bond Street is to London. It starts at Washington Arch [ABOVE] in Greenwich Village and is residential along its lower blocks. The city's most luxurious stores and hotels line the Avenue from the Empire State Building at 34 Street to the Hotel Plaza at 58th. Here are fashionable department stores such as Lord & Taylor, Best & Co. and Saks Fifth Avenue, the jewelers Cartier, Tiffany and Black, Starr & Gorham; F. A. O. Schwartz's gigantic toy store and the new Takashimaya Japanese store; the Steuben Glass showrooms; Brentano's, Scribner's and Doubleday bookstores, and the Gotham and St. Regis hotels.

THE FLATIRON BUILDING, Fifth Avenue, Broadway and 23 Street [LEFT] — New York's first skyscraper, this 21-story building was erected in 1902 and was for years the tallest in the city. Because of its peculiar shape, it was the most famous as well. The design — that of an old-fashioned flatiron — was dictated by its triangular plot of land. It was one of the first buildings to use modern steel-girder construction.

A GLASS BANK, Fifth Avenue and 43 Street [BELOW, LEFT] — This branch of the Manufacturer's Trust Company is a striking departure in bank architecture, replacing the traditional heavy, old-fashioned bank atmosphere with a delicate, open-to-the-world effect. Its huge vault can be seen from the street.

37

38

THE NEW YORK PUBLIC LIBRARY, Fifth Avenue, 40 to 42 Streets — One of the famous stone lions flanking the entrance to the Central Building of the New York Public Library. Opened in 1911, the massive marble structure, covering two city blocks, is the second-largest library in the United States. It contains four million volumes and is visited by more than 8,500 people each day.

BRYANT PARK — An oasis of quiet behind the New York Public Library, this small park is used as a summertime lunching spot by nearby office workers. Among its pleasant features is a noontime record concert piped from the Library. **40**

41

THE MUSEUM OF MODERN ART, 11 West 53 Street — Now one of New York's "old" landmarks, the Museum of Modern Art, built in 1939, specializes in the visual arts of the 20th century: painting, sculpture, architecture, industrial and commercial design, graphic arts, photography and motion pictures.

Visitors may lunch in the Museum restaurant, which overlooks the sculpture garden.

FIFTH AVENUE SHOPPING — Well-dressed women from all over America find the newest and smartest in the fashionable stores along Fifth Avenue [BELOW, RIGHT, the main floor of Bonwit Teller]. Display windows vie with one another to attract attention and convert window shoppers into indoor shoppers. At Christmas, as much imagination, time and money as go into the most elaborate stage or movie set go into the design of the Avenue's store windows. The whole shopping area becomes one long gallery of extravaganzas, and the show is so popular that some stores put up railings in front of their plate-glass windows to protect them from the crowds. Lord & Taylor [BELOW] is always one of the favorites.

43

4

45

THE FRICK COLLECTION, Fifth Avenue and 70 Street — Few of Fifth Avenue's palatial mansions remain. The Frick Collection was once the residence of the millionaire Henry Clay Frick, who left it, together with its immense art collection, to the public. The paintings, statuary and furnishings are not displayed as they usually are in a large museum but as they were when the Frick family lived there.

46

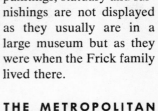

THE METROPOLITAN MUSEUM OF ART, Fifth Avenue at 82 Street — The most comprehensive collection of art in America is housed in a monumental building that sprawls along four blocks on Fifth Avenue. The art of 5,000 years is represented here in 234 separate galleries (fifteen rooms for their Egyptian collection alone).

Visitors may eat in the Museum restaurant, a soothing room with tables placed around a large pool which exhibits fountain sculpture by Carl Milles.

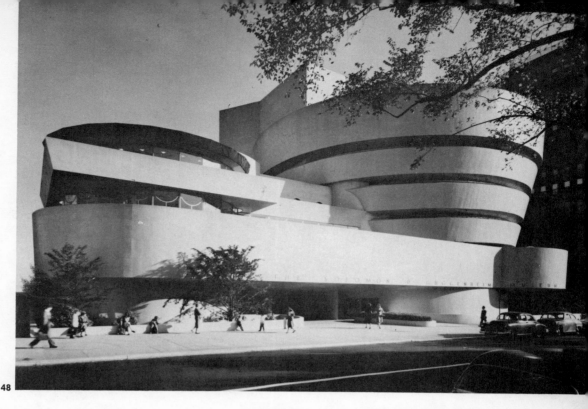

48

THE SOLOMON R. GUGGENHEIM MUSEUM, Fifth Avenue and 88 Street — One of the most arresting and controversial buildings in Manhattan (or in the world) is this museum designed by the late Frank Lloyd Wright. It was conceived as a giant spiral — one continuous floor in the form of a great winding ramp. This is a striking departure from the traditional museum architecture of separate room units. The effect of the gently slanting walls and special lighting innovations is to make the modern paintings on exhibit look as if they were floating, and not hung "square" on the walls. Visitors ride in an elevator to the top of the dome and then walk down the spiral at their leisure, viewing the paintings.

49

50

PARK AVENUE

Park Avenue now has two faces. Once entirely a residential area for the rich, its lower blocks have recently given way to huge glass-and-steel office buildings. Above 60 Street, the aura of "Millionaire's Row" is maintained: scrubbed sidewalks, green marquees and uniformed doormen with their imperious whistles summoning taxis for beautifully coiffed women with their beautifully coiffed poodles.

LEVER HOUSE, Park Avenue, 53 to 54 Streets — It is appropriate that a soap manufacturer should inhabit the cleanest-looking building in the city. A graceful small skyscraper, built entirely of glass and stainless steel, it has two employees whose full-time occupation is washing the exterior.

THE WALDORF-ASTORIA, Park Avenue, 49 to 50 Streets — Two pictures of the hotel where so many social functions are held that it is sometimes called the city's unofficial palace. One of the world's most luxurious hotels, it has a staff of 2,000 serving 2,200 rooms. The residential suites in the Waldorf Towers are the New York homes of such distinguished people as Adlai Stevenson, Douglas MacArthur, the Duke of Windsor and Cole Porter. Built over the tracks of the New York Central railroad, the hotel provides private sidings for those guests who travel on their own railway cars. A hotel tradition is to honor visiting dignitaries by displaying their flags; the photograph was taken outside the Park Avenue entrance on a day when both American and Russian diplomats were in residence.

56

THE SEAGRAM BUILDING, Park Avenue, 52 to 53 Streets —
Designed by Mies van der Rohe in bronze and glass, this 38-story
building is fronted by a generous half-acre plaza — a modern ver-
sion of the old-world feeling for space and dignity.

The Brasserie [LOWER RIGHT], in the Seagram Building, is open
twenty-four hours a day. Modeled after the French *brasseries*, it
is one of the few restaurants where a meal can be as simple as a
hamburger and a glass of red wine or as lavish as a seven-course
dinner with champagne. Prices are moderate, and the design, from
water glasses and silverware to the Picasso plaques on the walls, is
strikingly modern.

57

MIDTOWN

SMALL BUSINESS [LEFT] — Small mobile business establishments vending hot dogs and soft drinks and, in season, roasted chestnuts or ice cream, are seen all over.

ESCALATORS [BELOW, LEFT] — Very little stair-climbing need be done in transportation terminals, subways and department stores. Here is a rush-hour scene at the Port Authority Bus Terminal, one of the busiest commuting centers.

DIG WE MUST [BELOW] — A familiar sight at any time, anywhere, is the Consolidated Edison Company crew repairing pipes and wires just under the city's surface. Their apologetic motto: Dig we must — for growing New York.

THE BUSIEST CITY IN THE WORLD [RIGHT] — A triple exposure dramatizing frenetic midtown activity that is New York's and New York's alone.

AFTER DARK — Year after year, as more new glass buildings go up, the city becomes brighter and brighter after dark, when the cleaning staff takes over.

FIRE ESCAPES — One of the first things to catch the eye of the visitor from abroad is the profusion of exterior fire escapes on the old buildings.

THE AUTOMAT [ABOVE] — Children are fascinated by the Automat. Put the coins in the slot and turn the handle; the little glass door opens, and there's your sandwich. There are 38 Horn & Hardart Automats in the city.

LE CAFE CHAMBORD, Third Avenue between 49 and 50 Streets [ABOVE, RIGHT] — For twenty-five years New York's Le Café Chambord has represented the classic French cuisine. Luxurious, leisurely and expensive, each table has the services of a captain, two waiters, a busboy and, most probably, the wine steward. Here a captain gives the final touches to a specialty of the house, *Caneton Bigarade Flambé.*

ART GALLERY [RIGHT] — The opening of a show at an art gallery on 57 Street. Hundreds of galleries are concentrated along this street and on upper Madison Avenue. The gentleman in the foreground is part of the exhibit, not part of the cocktail party.

"MEET ME UNDER THE CLOCK" [RIGHT] — As popular a meeting place for today's college crowd as it was for their fathers and mothers is "under the clock" in the lobby of the Biltmore Hotel at Madison Avenue and 43 Street.

THE WORLD'S LARGEST STORE — Macy's, at Broadway and 34 Street, is the world's largest store. It carries a stock of more than 400,000 items from all over the world, has 11,000 employees and averages 150,000 customers a day. Each year Macy's sponsors a Fourth of July fireworks display on the Hudson River and a Thanksgiving Day parade. The parade, here seen passing through Times Square, has been an elaborate event for the past thirty-four years: giant balloon figures, floats, clowns, bands and guest celebrities from the movies and TV.

71

72

THE GARMENT CENTER, Sixth to Ninth Avenues, 30 to 42 Streets — Traffic and
confusion, trucks loading and unloading, pushboys guiding hand trucks bright with
dresses and workers discussing business on the sidewalk during noon hour — the
Garment Center, site of New York's most important industry.

NEW YORK COLISEUM, Columbus Circle — This thirty-five-million-dollar convention and exhibition hall holds over a hundred shows annually and can accommodate
as many as 35,000 people.

73

EL MOROCCO, 307 East 54 Street — The club that the society and gossip columnists couldn't exist without. Celebrities and the elite go here to look at one another. When John Perona opened this smart supper club in 1931 he cannily established his hallmark, zebra-striped upholstery — thus insuring that the El Morocco would be immediately recognized as the setting when photographs of celebrities appeared in the newspapers.

COPACABANA, 10 East 60 Street — Known familiarly as "The Copa," this large, plush cellar headlines big-name stars of the entertainment world and a famous line of pretty girls. Two orchestras alternate for dancing.

NIGHT CLUBS

The variety and excitement of New York night life is second only to that of Paris. Night clubbers can find everything from inexpensive Egyptian cabarets to red-plush, white-tie-and-tails supper clubs. The cost can run anywhere from $3.00 to an arm and a leg.

UPSTAIRS AT THE DOWNSTAIRS, 37 West 56 Street [ABOVE] — The cabaret review is of fairly recent vintage. This is a traditional opening curtain, complete with cast, of Julius Monk's Upstairs at the Downstairs. Mr. Monk runs an equally sophisticated sister show on the floor below in a room called, logically enough, Downstairs at the Upstairs.

BASIN STREET EAST, 137 East 48 Street — The biggest names in the jazz world entertain at this club. Peggy Lee sings and Jimmy Durante is a guest at a ringside table.

EDDIE CONDON'S, 330 East 56 Street — The best-known dixieland-jazz club belongs to the durable Eddie Condon (far left), who recently moved uptown after many years as a Greenwich Village fixture.

79

81

THE UNITED NATIONS First Avenue, 42 to 48 Streets

Built in 1952 on eighteen acres of land donated by John D. Rockefeller, Jr., the permanent headquarters of the United Nations is a major tourist attraction. On the left, seen from the East River, is the Secretariat Building and the oddly shaped General Assembly Building. (On their right is the Chrysler Building.) Visitors have technically left United States territory once they enter the UN grounds.

The flags of the 99 member nations [ABOVE] fly outside the 39-story Secretariat Building, which is entirely windows on both sides — 5,400 of them. The main public entrance [TOP LEFT] is in the General Assembly Building. The balconies at left lead to the public galleries of the Assembly Hall.

THE PUBLIC GALLERY [LEFT] in the Security Council Chamber. Earphones wired to a telephone-dial system are provided at each seat. Speeches are generally interpreted simultaneously in the official languages—Chinese, English, French, Russian and Spanish.

THE SECURITY COUNCIL CHAMBER [LEFT] donated to the UN by Norway. The room was decorated by Arnstein Arneberg, and the striking mural is by Per Krohg.

TOURS [RIGHT] of the main buildings and meeting rooms are conducted on regular schedules. The attractive guides represent many nations, and among them speak some 24 languages.

THE GENERAL ASSEMBLY HALL [BELOW] — There are 830 seats for delegates, 270 for observers, 234 for the press and 816 for the public. The murals were designed by the French artist Fernand Léger.

84

CENTRAL PARK

59 to 110 Streets, Fifth Avenue
to Central Park West

THIRTY-FIVE MILES OF FOOTPATH ramble through the park. This quiet spot reflects the hotels on Central Park South and Fifth Avenue.

HANS CHRISTIAN ANDERSEN STATUE, near Fifth Avenue and 74 Street — The children's storytelling center was erected in 1956 and was a gift to the city from Danish school children. Children are encouraged both to look at it and climb on it.

In 1856, when the city purchased the land for Central Park, the 840-acre area was called, in a contemporary document, "a bare, unsightly and disgusting spot." Then the outskirts of the city, it was rocky, sparsely vegetated land with a handful of squatters' shacks. Careful development and intelligent landscaping have turned it into one of the world's most beautiful recreation areas.

Looking at it from the south [BELOW], we see the two-and-a-half-mile stretch of luxury hotels and apartment houses rimming the park along Fifth Avenue, Central Park South and Central Park West. The 100-acre Receiving Reservoir (which stores water from upstate) is at the north end of the park, and just below it on Fifth Avenue, is the Metropolitan Museum of Art.

Looking over Central Park is the city's finest old hotel, the dignified and elegant Plaza [RIGHT], built in 1907. The most elaborate debutante and charity balls are traditionally held in its Grand Ballroom. It is situated on the Grand Army Plaza, one of the city's most refreshing open spaces.

THE LUXURY OF GRASS amid the city's concrete and steel is invitation to a siesta.

89

THE POND near the Plaza entrance is next to a fenced-in wildlife preserve. In season, it is a favorite stopping-off place for migratory birds.

90

BRIDLE PATH — Horses may be rented by the hour from the stables a few blocks west of the park. There are six miles of bridle path.

NATURAL ROCK FORMA-TIONS have been worked into the landscaping of the park, providing exciting "mountain climbing" for young explorers.

92

SPORTS: The park provides football fields, baseball diamonds, tennis courts, rowboating and a yacht basin for miniature boats.

93

THE ZOO, entrance at Fifth Avenue and 64 Street — Feeding time for the seals (about 1:30) is a fine free show. The Central Park Zoo is small, but it contains all the customary animals. In the background is the cafeteria, pleasant for outdoor lunch during the warm months.

94

95

HORSE-DRAWN CARRIAGES take visitors on leisurely rides through the park, starting from the Grand Army Plaza.

WOLLMAN MEMORIAL RINK, an artificial ice-skating rink during the winter, is used for roller skating and dancing in the summer.

UPPER NEW YORK

THE GEORGE WASHINGTON BRIDGE — Completed in 1931, this graceful bridge soars over the Hudson River connecting upper Manhattan and New Jersey. Just short of a mile long, it is the second-longest suspension bridge in the world (San Francisco's Golden Gate ranks first).

THE CLOISTERS [RIGHT], Fort Tryon Park, 190 Street — The Cloisters, a skillful reconstruction of a medieval monastery, is situated on a rocky ridge overlooking the Hudson. Incorporated into the structure are sections from medieval buildings brought over from Europe: a 12th-century chapter house, a Romanesque chapel and parts of five different French cloisters dating from the 12th to the 15th centuries. The building also houses a fine collection of medieval art.

101

102

CATHEDRAL OF ST. JOHN THE DIVINE, Amsterdam Avenue and 112 Street [LEFT] — Eventually, this unfinished Gothic cathedral (Protestant Episcopal), which has been in construction for over sixty years, will be the largest church building in America and the largest Gothic cathedral in the world. Now about two-thirds finished, there is no way of knowing when it will see completion, since it is being added to only as money becomes available.

GRANT'S TOMB AND RIVERSIDE CHURCH, Riverside Drive and 122 Street — Grant's Tomb is missed by few tourists; few New Yorkers have ever been inside. Mural maps of battles and regimental battle flags of the Civil War are exhibited in rooms off the rotunda.

The interdenominational Riverside Church has the distinction of having the world's largest carillon at the top of its 22-story tower. The 74 bells were given by John D. Rockefeller in memory of his mother. The church, French Gothic in style, is noted for its beautiful stained-glass windows.

THE AMERICAN MUSEUM OF NATURAL HISTORY, Central Park West at 79 Street [LEFT] — Skeletons of prehistoric animals; models of insect, fossil, animal and floral life; and a graphic exhibit of the development of man are all to be seen in this museum, the largest of its kind in the world. The Hayden Planetarium gives an exciting visual representation of the moon, stars and the universe.

YORKVILLE — New York's German colony is in Yorkville, which centers around East 86 Street. German is heard on the streets; there is a German-language movie theater and an abundance of delicatessens, pork stores, restaurants and music halls. The audience participates in the Bavarian show [RIGHT] at the 86 Street Brauhaus.

To the east of Yorkville is Gracie Mansion, the official home of the mayor, and Carl Schurz Park [BELOW], which runs along the East River for five blocks.

105

LEWISOHN STADIUM, City College Campus, Amsterdam Avenue and 138 Street — Summer concerts under the stars, with only an occasional interruption from airplanes overhead, are presented by the finest symphony orchestras and soloists.

FREEDOMLAND — Just north of Manhattan, on what was mostly swampland, there now sprawls a 205-acre entertainment center, constructed in the topographical form of the United States. Within it are authentic re-creations of settings from the American past — Little Old New York, San Francisco's Barbary Coast — and a costumed cast of hundreds who re-enact such Americana as political rallies and cowboy-and-Indian skirmishes. Picturesque sternwheelers paddle along the "Great Lakes."

YANKEE STADIUM, River Avenue and 161 Street — The largest sports arena in the city, Yankee Stadium seats 70,000. It is the home of the New York Yankees, but is frequently used for major boxing and football attractions as well as baseball.

THE BRONX ZOO — Over a thousand different species of animals, birds and reptiles are exhibited in America's largest zoo. Opened in 1899, it is particularly noted for a number of rare specimens — platypuses, okapis and quetzals. In the Children's Zoo, no adult is admitted unless accompanied by a child. A large variety of animals roam together in amity on the African Plains, landscaped to resemble their natural habitat.

109

110

The largest Negro community in America is crowded into an area of approximately three square miles. Although it is still the worst slum area in the city, low-rent housing developments are gradually clearing away block after block. 125 Street is the main thoroughfare for shopping and entertainment.

Following World War II, about half a million Puerto Ricans came to the city, most of them settling around the edges of Harlem and in neighborhoods which earlier waves of immigration had vacated. At the first sign of warm weather, social activity moves outdoors to the front steps of brownstone houses and the sidewalks. With the Puerto Ricans came colorful *bodegas* or groceries, store-front churches, and open-air preachers, some of whom are accompanied by their own instrumental combinations.

111

112

PUBLIC MARKET, Park Avenue and 110 to 116 Streets — Shoppers from all over the city come to these swarming, noisy markets, housed in a series of six block-long sheds. Many of the fruits and vegetables, sold to the residents of the near-by Puerto Rican neighborhoods, would be considered by the average American to be exotic and unusual.

HARLEM

110 to 145 Streets, East River to Hudson River

GREENWICH VILLAGE

Greenwich Village is a jumble of old houses, new buildings, twisting streets and a confusion of geography. It extends some fifteen blocks south of 14 Street and from the Hudson River crosstown to Broadway. Known as the home of bohemians and beatniks, artists and writers (authentic and unauthentic), it is where young people gather to try out their individuality.

Everyone who visits New York or lives in the city spends time in the Village. The attractions are many: a variety of unusual, inexpensive restaurants, coffeehouses, honky-tonk night clubs, offbeat specialty shops, paperback bookstores, and interesting people to look at.

WASHINGTON SQUARE PARK — Washington Arch, which commemorates the inauguration of the first President, is at the foot of Fifth Avenue. Especially on warm weekends, social activity in in Greenwich Village centers around the circular fountain. When filled with water it is a children's wading pool; when dry it is a favorite sunning spot and frequently the scene of as many as seven or eight simultaneous folk-song concerts.

WASHINGTON SQUARE ART SHOW [BELOW] — During the months of June and September artists turn Washington Square into an outdoor gallery. Exhibits of paintings and sculpture rim the square and flow off onto the side streets.

116

THE VILLAGE'S MAIN STREET is Eighth Street — two blocks of small specialty shops, big bookstores, movie theaters, bars and restaurants.

120

BEATNIKS, BOHEMIANS AND TOURISTS — MacDougal Street on a Saturday night brings out the beatniks, the Village characters and the tourists. On the stretch between West Third and Bleecker Streets are restaurants, bars, coffeehouses, a folklore center and shops selling handmade jewelry and leathercraft.

COFFEEHOUSES have sprung up in abundance in the last five years. Some are for quiet conversation, others for poetry readings and folk-song sessions.

121

OFF-BROADWAY THEATER — In converted lofts, bars and church basements seating anywhere from 25 to 300, the theater-goer can take his choice of anything from Shakespeare to the most avant-garde drama. The actors are virtually surrounded by their audience at The Premise, famous for improvisational theater.

WASHINGTON MEWS [RIGHT] — Half a block above Washington Square, running from Fifth Avenue to University Place, is a privately owned cobbled street whose charming houses and studios are converted stables.

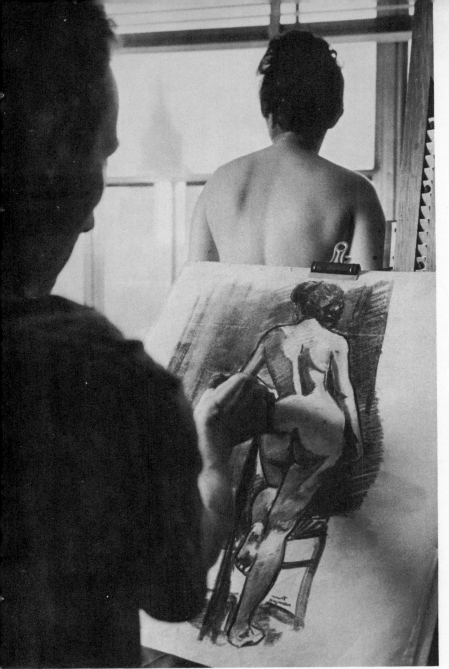

ARTIST'S STUDIO [LEFT] — The artists live and work in everything from low-rent lofts to high-rent, high-ceilinged studios. A shadowy Empire State Building can be seen through the window of artist Mort Hyman's studio.

SIDEWALK CAFE [BELOW, LEFT] — A Village restaurant with "atmosphere" is this converted butcher shop on the corner of Avenue of the Americas and Fourth Street. The meat hooks are still on the walls at O. Henry's, and there is sawdust on the floor. The waiters dress in traditional butcher costume — white smocks and straw hats. It is especially popular for its outdoor café.

THE OLD AND THE NEW VILLAGE [BELOW] — Some of the old houses remain, but there is an air of doom about them as new buildings spring up at their sides.

LUCHOW'S, 110 East 14 Street [LEFT] — Luchow's German restaurant was established in its present location — now an unfashionable one — in 1882, and it still retains its spacious dignity. Viennese waltzes are background music at dinner.

GRAMERCY PARK, Lexington Avenue to University Place, 20 to 21 Streets — a private park resembling many in London. It was laid out in 1831 by a real-estate man who felt that wealthy families would appreciate quiet and exclusiveness in the center of a city that was noisy even then. Access to the park is only by keys (originally made of gold) furnished to the residents.

128

Surrounding the Park are some of the most graceful houses in the city, a few with delicate wrought-iron porches. In this picture is one of the two "Mayor's Lamps" outside Number 4 Gramercy Park West. By long custom these lamps were placed in front of the home of the mayor; Number 4 was the home of James Harper, mayor from 1884 to 1885. Among the famous buildings rimming the Park are the National Arts Club, The Players (an actors' club) and the Friends Meeting House.

129

THE LITTLE CHURCH AROUND THE CORNER, 1 East 29 Street — More marriages are performed here at the Bride's Altar than at any other church in the city. Officially known as the Church of the Transfiguration (Protestant Episcopal), it was given its other, more familiar name in 1870, when the minister of a conservative Madison Avenue church refused to hold burial services for an actor, suggesting that the family of the deceased "try the little church around the corner, where they don't mind actors." Theater people have been in heavy attendance ever since.

THE FINANCIAL DISTRICT

THE NEW YORK STOCK EXCHANGE, Broad and Wall Streets [LEFT] — The exterior of the Stock Exchange, as seen from behind the statue of George Washington on the steps of the Sub-Treasury Building, where he took his oath of office as first president.

WALL STREET [BELOW] is the money center of the world.

What appears to be chaos on the floor of one of the largest rooms in the world is the Stock Exchange in action. Here stocks and bonds (of 1,200 companies) are traded, bought and sold in an amazingly informal fashion. Stockbrokers must own a "seat" on the Exchange (worth $225,000) in order to trade on the floor. Orders to buy or sell are relayed by telephone from their brokerage firms, and business is transacted verbally with the traders stationed behind the horse-shoe-shaped trading posts. Transactions are immediately recorded on the ticker tape and telegraphed around the world.

A dizzying view of the Wall Street area [BELOW, RIGHT]. The skyscraper in the center is the new 64-story Chase Manhattan Bank Building, whose boundaries are Nassau, Liberty, Pine and William Streets.

TICKER TAPE PARADE PASSING TRINITY CHURCH — Ticker-tape parades honoring visiting dignitaries are a New York tradition. Here a procession passes Trinity Church, at the corner of Broadway and Wall Street. The present church, beautifully proportioned in the Gothic Revival mode, was completed in 1846, and was for 52 years the tallest building in the city. Many of the graves in the churchyard date back to 1698, the year in which the first Trinity Church was erected on this site.

135

UPTOWN FROM DOWNTOWN — A view north from the Cities Service Building (also known as 60 Wall Tower).

136

NASSAU STREET [BELOW] — The city's busiest noon-hour pedestrian traffic is on Nassau Street. Quick-service restaurants and discount stores attract so many office workers that it is almost impossible for a car to make its way through the narrow street with its overflowing sidewalks.

138

WALL STREET CANYONS — The immense value of land in the financial district has dictated that the buildings be tall and narrow — thus the famous "Wall Street Canyons."

U. S. CUSTOM HOUSE [BELOW] — The architecture of 1907 and the architecture of 1960 in typical contrast — the U. S. Custom House and Number 2 Broadway.

37

139

140

141

BROOKLYN BRIDGE, Park Row, east of City Hall — The opening of the Brooklyn Bridge in 1883 was a national holiday. This first bridge across the East River was considered the greatest engineering achievement of the 19th century and the eighth wonder of the world. Its graceful lines have been the delight of painters, photographers and poets. It was built with pedestrians mainly in mind — they paid a penny to walk across — but has long since become one of the chief arteries for vehicular and subway traffic between lower New York and Brooklyn.

THE BATTERY — Battery Park and the harbor. The circular structure in the park was originally a fort — Castle Clinton, erected in 1807. Over the succeeding years it became, as Castle Garden, a center for social and public events (Jenny Lind sang there), an immigration station, and the site of the New York Aquarium. The Aquarium was recently moved to Coney Island.

142

143

144

THE WOOLWORTH BUILDING, Broadway and Park Place — Just south of City Hall Park is the soaring 60-story Woolworth Building, erected in 1913. For almost two decades it was the tallest and most talked-about building in the world. The aim of its architect, Cass Gilbert, was to erect a Gothic "cathedral of commerce." Although it is now only the seventh-tallest skyscraper in Manhattan, there are many who believe that it remains the most architecturally pleasing.

STATEN ISLAND FERRY — The five-cent ferry ride from the Battery to Staten Island is the city's best bargain. The harbor activity is always interesting, and the skyline view from the ferry is the most celebrated of all.

CITY HALL — This beautifully proportioned civic building, completed in 1811, is an American Colonial adaptation of French Renaissance architecture.

147

FULTON FISH MARKET, South Street from Fulton Street to Brooklyn Bridge [ABOVE] — In the early morning — from 3:00 until 9:00 or 10:00 — this old and battered part of the city is the scene of frenetic activity. Tons of fish — well over 100 varieties — are unloaded from refrigerated trucks and weather-beaten trawlers, processed, and shipped out to restaurants and stores.

Sloppy Louie's restaurant, which is not *really* sloppy, opens at five in the morning to serve sea-food breakfasts to the fishmongers, market workers, and the few adventurous tourists who have been to see the fish market in action.

146

THE BOWERY from Chatham Square to East Fourth Street — New York's seamiest side is here. A floating population of alcoholics and unemployables; a string of pawn shops and flophouses, missions, barber colleges and saloons.

148

149

LOWER EAST SIDE — The Lower East Side extends from 14 Street south to Canal Street and from Broadway to the East River. Wave after wave of immigrants have settled in its crowded tenements for over a century. The Germans and the Irish have long since moved on; hundreds of thousands of Jewish immigrants characterized the Lower East Side for decades. Today, only the older generation is in evidence, sharing the area with the new wave of Puerto Ricans. On Sunday, the outdoor markets on Orchard Street are at their busiest.

150

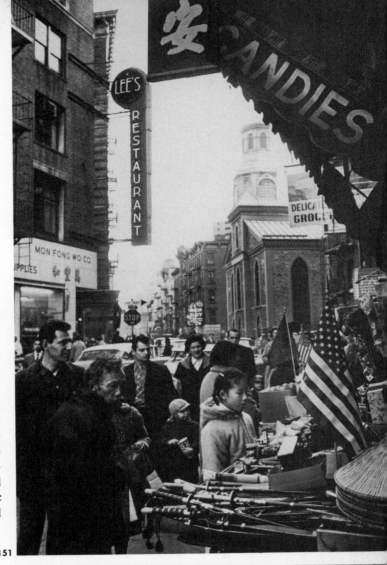

CHINATOWN — Six thousand Chinese live in this small triangular area, whose principal streets are Mott, Pell and Doyers. It is the shopping center for another forty thousand Chinese in the metropolitan area. In these winding streets are dozens of fine Cantonese restaurants. The grocery-shop windows with their fascinating displays of unusual vegetables, herbs and exotic dried fish are worth a special journey.

151

BIG BUSINESS like this is still transacted from the Lower East Side's few remaining pushcarts.

IN THE OPPRESSIVE HEAT OF SUMMER [BELOW] children in the crowded neighborhoods cool off by opening the fire hydrants — sometimes with official permission, sometimes not.

LITTLE ITALY [ABOVE] — The city's oldest Italian neighborhood is concentrated along Mulberry Street. Scenes such as this might make a visitor believe he is in the back streets of Naples.

SAN GENNARO FESTIVAL [RIGHT] — The largest and gaudiest Italian street festival is the Feast of San Gennaro during the week of September 19th. Colored lights are strung over five blocks of Mulberry Street and a statue of the saint is carried in a procession. The area is jammed with people, and the music is loud. There are gambling booths and stalls selling pizza, clams, hot sausage and cheese-stuffed calzone.

155

CONEY ISLAND — Ten miles from Times Square is Brooklyn's Coney Island, the Honky-tonk by the Sea. An estimated forty-five million people visit its crowded beach and amusement park each year. There are ferris wheels, roller coasters, fun houses, freak shows and shooting galleries. It is famed as the home of the hot dog.

A relatively uncrowded portion of the beach, showing the 250-foot parachute jump.

BROOKLYN HEIGHTS — Brooklyn Heights, directly across the East River from lower Manhattan, is a quiet, distinguished residential neighborhood. Its Esplanade looks out across the East River to New York's financial district. The bottom of Wall Street is roughly in the center of the picture.

158

CLOVER LEAF — To control the heavy traffic pouring into the city, the highways are laid out in complicated clover-leaf patterns.

Tugboats nudging the *Queen Elizabeth* into her Hudson River dock.

EXITS AND ENTRANCES

PENNSYLVANIA STATION, Seventh to Eighth Avenues, 31 to 33 Streets [LEFT] — The world's largest railroad terminal was completed in 1910. The architects modeled it after a Roman bath. It covers 28 acres and handles one hundred million people each year; four railway lines use it as a terminus. This photo shows the glass-domed concourse. The new Madison Square Garden sports arena will be built above the station.

GRAND CENTRAL TERMINAL, Park Avenue at 42 Street [BELOW] — Before advertising displays took over, the huge marble concourse was one of the most dignified and impressive sights in New York. The vaulted blue ceiling represents the heavens, with blinking stars and tracings of the signs of the zodiac.

163

NEW YORK INTERNATIONAL AIRPORT (IDLEWILD) — The world's largest commercial airport handles some seven million passengers each year. Opened in 1948, it covers five thousand acres.

Above, on the right, is the recently completed eleven-block-long International Arrival Building.

The Pan American World Airways Terminal [RIGHT] is designed so that passengers boarding and leaving planes may be sheltered by the overhanging roof.

FUTURES

"New York will be a wonderful place if they ever finish it."

The city is going through the biggest construction boom in its history. There are holes in the ground and men in the sky all over Manhattan; the streets are loud with the incessant noise of drilling and blasting, and the silhouettes of steel girders change from day to day.

THE PAN AM BUILDING, 200 Park Avenue [BELOW] — The world's largest commercial office building is scheduled for completion in December 1962. The hundred-million-dollar, 59-story octagonal structure will adjoin Grand Central Station.

TWO HUGE LUXURY HOTELS are going up a block apart from each other just above Times Square. The New York Hilton [UPPER RIGHT] on Avenue of the Americas between 53 and 54 Streets (early 1963) will have 43 stories and 2,150 rooms. The crescent-shaped Americana of New York [RIGHT] on Seventh Avenue between 52 and 53 Streets (mid-1962) will be the world's tallest hotel — 50 stories — and will have 2,000 rooms.

170

172

THE GALLERY OF MODERN ART, Columbus Circle [LEFT] — A new museum, devoted exclusively to the art of the 19th and 20th centuries, is scheduled for completion in the spring of 1962. The nine-story building, designed by Edward Durrell Stone, will overlook Central Park. It will be built with the funds provided by Huntington Hartford.

THE HARTFORD PAVILION [BELOW] — In the near future the city will blossom with an outdoor café on the southeast corner of Central Park. The café has been donated to the city by Huntington Hartford, who felt that New York needed a place "gay, accessible, ornamental, and within the means of the average family and tourist." At street level, facing the Plaza, there will be fifty tables. The tables on the lower level will look out on Central Park Pond.

Amsterdam to Columbus Avenues, West 62 to West 66 Streets.
Scale model of Lincoln Center. Clockwise from the left, the buildings and the architects who designed them are: New York State Theater for the Dance and Operetta (Philip Johnson Associates); Damrosch Park and Guggenheim Band Shell; Metropolitan Opera House (Wallace K. Harrison); Library-Museum (Skidmore, Owings & Merrill), in which is housed the Repertory Drama Theater (Eero Saarinen with Jo Mielziner as collaborating designer); Juilliard School of Music (Pietro Belluschi); and Philharmonic Hall (Max Abramovitz). Chief architect for the entire project is Wallace K. Harrison.

LINCOLN CENTER FOR THE PERFORMING ARTS — The largest cultural project ever conceived in America is scheduled for completion in 1964, in time for the World's Fair. Philharmonic Hall will open in 1962, and other buildings as they are completed. Eight auditoriums with an estimated seating capacity of 12,000 will be the focal point for opera, ballet, symphony and drama in New York City. The 20-story tower behind the Metropolitan Opera House will dominate the complex and will be used for scenery storage, workshops and offices for Lincoln Center. The music, dance and drama collections of the New York Public Library will be housed in the Library-Museum, and there will be an underground garage for 750 cars.

THE VERRAZANO-NARROWS BRIDGE — When completed in 1965, this will be the world's longest suspension span — nearly three miles. It will cross The Narrows, the entrance to New York Harbor, and will connect Brooklyn and Staten Island, affording a New York City by-pass for traffic along the Eastern seaboard. It is named after the Florentine navigator Giovanni da Verrazano, who first sailed into New York Harbor in 1524.

NEW YORK WORLD'S FAIR 1964-1965 — Drawing of the Unisphere, a 135-foot-high globe of stainless steel. Every continent will be seen from any viewpoint, dramatizing the theme of the Fair — that all nations are closer together and must work for unity in the world today.

Unisphere is presented by United States (U_S S) Steel Corporation.

The Fair will be held on 646 acres of Flushing Meadow Park. The estimated attendance is seventy million.

PICTURE CREDITS

The editors wish to express their indebtedness to the many organizations that have helped with information and photographs. We are particularly grateful to five photographers whose enthusiastic co-operation went beyond the call of duty: William Hubbell, Peter Lacey, Seymour Linden, C. B. Crumpton and Richard L. Grossman. And our thanks to Eve Metz for her interest and imaginative skill in designing the book.

NOTE: *The numbers referred to in the Picture Credits are photograph numbers*

Cover, Port of New York Authority
1 PETER LACEY
2 FRITZ HENLE, courtesy Cities Service Co.
3 Fairchild Aerial Surveys, Inc.
4 Fairchild Aerial Surveys, Inc.
5 Port of New York Authority
6 Port of New York Authority
7 BURT GLINN, Magnum Photos
8, 9, 10 Empire State Building Corp.
11 WILLIAM HUBBELL
12 C. B. CRUMPTON, Cornet
13 ERNST HAAS, Magnum Photos
14 PETER LACEY
15, 16 WILLIAM HUBBELL
17 PETER LACEY
18 WILLIAM HUBBELL
19 Courtesy the Latin Quarter
20 Courtesy Lindy's Restaurant
21 PETER LACEY
22 Courtesy Department of Commerce and Public Events
23 Thomas Airviews, Courtesy Rockefeller Center, Inc.
24 RICHARD H. ALTHOFF, Courtesy Rockefeller Center, Inc.
25 MAUREY GARBER, Courtesy Rockefeller Center, Inc.
26 EDWARD RATCLIFFE, Courtesy Rockefeller Center, Inc.
27 RICHARD L. GROSSMAN
28 Courtesy Radio City Music Hall
29 HENRY RAPISARDA, Cosmo Sileo Inc., Courtesy Radio City Music Hall
30 National Broadcasting Corp.
31 JOHN HUGELMEYER, Courtesy Restaurant Associates
32 WILLIAM HUBBELL
33 TOMMY WEBER, Courtesy Union News Co.
34 SEYMOUR LINDEN
35 RICHARD L. GROSSMAN
36 WILLIAM HUBBELL
37 PETER LACEY
38 EZRA STOLLER, Courtesy Manufacturers Trust Co.
39 WILLIAM HUBBELL
40 MAUREY GARBER, Courtesy New York Public Library
41 RICHARD L. GROSSMAN
42 Courtesy Museum of Modern Art
43 SEYMOUR LINDEN
44 Courtesy Lord & Taylor
45 SEYMOUR LINDEN
46 Copyright The Frick Collection, New York
47 Courtesy of Metropolitan Museum of Art

48, 49 EZRA STOLLER, Courtesy Solomon R. Guggenheim Museum
50 Courtesy Solomon R. Guggenheim Museum
51 PETER LACEY
52 C. B. CRUMPTON, Cornet
53 Courtesy Lever House
54, 55 WILL WEISSBERG, Courtesy Waldorf-Astoria
56 EZRA STOLLER, Courtesy Seagram Building
57 DAVID WORKMAN, Courtesy Restaurant Associates
58 C. B. CRUMPTON, Cornet
59 The New York Convention & Visitors Bureau
60 Courtesy Consolidated Edison Corp.
61 WILLIAM HUBBELL
62 EZRA STOLLER, Courtesy Lever House
63 ROY HYRKIN
64 PETER LACEY
65 SEYMOUR LINDEN
66, 67 PETER LACEY
68, 69, 70 Courtesy R. H. Macy and Co.
71, 72 LIDA MOSER
73 Courtesy New York Coliseum
74 Courtesy El Morocco
75 Courtesy Jules Podell's Copacabana
76 WERNER J. KUHN, Courtesy Upstairs at the Downstairs
77 Courtesy Basin Street East
78 Courtesy Eddie Condon's
79-84A Courtesy United Nations
85 BRUCE DAVIDSON, Magnum Photos
86, 87 WILLIAM HUBBELL
88 Ewing Galloway, Courtesy Rockefeller Center, Inc.
89 PETER LACEY
90, 91, 92 SEYMOUR LINDEN
93, 94, 95, 96 PETER LACEY
97 ANN ZANE SHANKS
98 WILLIAM HUBBELL
99 PETER LACEY
100 Courtesy Cities Service Co.
101 PETER LACEY
102 Courtesy of American Museum of Natural History
103 C. B. CRUMPTON, Cornet
104 ANN ZANE SHANKS
105 HANS W. SCHOENLANK, Courtesy of 86th Street Brauhaus
106 FRED A. HAMEL, Courtesy Stadium Concerts Inc.
107 Courtesy Freedomland
108 Courtesy New York Yankees
109 PETER LACEY
110 Courtesy New York Zoological Society
111 ROY HYRKIN
112 PAUL DUCKWORTH, P. I. P.
113 HARRY HESS
114 WILLIAM HUBBELL
115 HARRY HESS
116 PETER LACEY
117 GIN BRIGGS
118, 119 SEYMOUR LINDEN
120, 121 PETER LACEY
122 MAX WALDMAN, Courtesy The Premise
123, 124 SEYMOUR LINDEN
125 DAVID WORKMAN, Courtesy O. Henry's Steak House
126 WILLIAM HUBBELL
127, 128, 129 PETER LACEY
130 New York Convention & Visitors Bureau
131, 132 WILLIAM HUBBELL
133 ERICH HARTMANN, Magnum Photos

134 Fairchild Aerial Surveys, Inc.
135 BURT GLINN, Magnum Photos
136 FRITZ HENLE, Courtesy Cities Service Co.
137 Wide World Photos
138, 139, 140 PETER LACEY
141 LIDA MOSER
142 ELLIOTT ERWITT, Magnum Photos
143 Courtesy Parker-Brand Corp.
144 C. B. CRUMPTON, Cornet
145 PETER LACEY
146 HARRY HESS
147 C. B. CRUMPTON, Cornet
148, 149 SEYMOUR LINDEN
150 ROY HYRKIN
151 PETER LACEY
152 Wide World Photos
153 WEEGEE, P. I. P.
154 ROY HYRKIN
155 GIN BRIGGS
156 WEEGEE, P. I. P.
157 ERNST HAAS, Magnum Photos
158 PETER LACEY
159 WILLIAM HUBBELL
160 Fairchild Aerial Surveys, Inc.
161, 162 WILLIAM HUBBELL
163 C. B. CRUMPTON, Cornet
164 Port of New York Authority
165 Courtesy Pan American World Airways
166 C. B. CRUMPTON, Cornet
167 RICHARD L. GROSSMAN
168, 169 ROBERT LAWRENCE PASTNER, Courtesy Uris Buildings Corp.
170 Courtesy Pan American World Airways
171 Courtesy Uris Buildings Corp.
172 Courtesy Loew's Theatres, Inc.
173, 174 LOUIS CHECKMAN, Courtesy Edward Durrell Stone
175 Maris—Ezra Stoller Associates, Courtesy Lincoln Center for the Performing Arts
176 Triborough Bridge and Tunnel Authority
177 N. Y. World's Fair 1964-1965 Corp.

INDEX

NOTE: *The numbers referred to in the Index are photograph numbers*

American Museum of Natural History 102
Americana of New York 172
Automat 64
Basin Street East 77
Battery Park 142
Bowery, The 148
Brasserie, The 57
Bronx Zoo 109
Brooklyn Bridge 141
Brooklyn Heights 158
Bryant Park 39
Cathedral of St. John the Divine 101
Central Park 88
Central Park Zoo 94
Chambord, Le Cafe 65
Chinatown 151
City Hall 145
Cloisters, The 99
Coney Island 156
Copacabana 75
Eddie Condon's 78
Eighty-sixth Street Brauhaus 105
El Morocco 74

Empire State Building 8
Fifth Avenue 36
Financial District 131
Flatiron Building 37
Freedomland 107
Frick Collection 46
Fulton Fish Market 147
Gallery of Modern Art 173
Garment District 71
George Washington Bridge 98
Gramercy Park 128
Grand Central Terminal 163
Grant's Tomb 103
Greenwich Village 116
Guggenheim Museum 48
Harlem 111
Hartford Pavilion 174
Idlewild 166
Information Center 22
La Fonda del Sol 31
Latin Quarter 19
Lever House 53
Lewisohn Stadium 106
Lincoln Center for the Performing Arts 175
Lindy's 20
Little Church Around the Corner 130
Louis XIV, Cafe 33
Lower East Side 150
Luchow's 127
MacDougal Street 120
Macy's 68
Metropolitan Museum of Art 47
Mulberry Street 154
Museum of Modern Art 41
Nassau Street 137
New York Coliseum 73
New York Hilton 171
New York International Airport 166
New York Public Library 40
New York Stock Exchange 133
New York World's Fair 1964-1965 177
O. Henry's Steak House 125
Olivetti 35
Outdoor Art Show 117
Palladium 21
Pan Am Building 170
Pan American World Airways Terminal 165
Park Avenue 51
Pennsylvania Station 162
Plaza Hotel 87
Premise, The 122
Radio City Music Hall 28
Riverside Church 103
Rockefeller Center 23
Rockefeller Center Outdoor Ice Skating Pond 27
Rockettes 29
St. Patrick's Cathedral 32
San Gennaro Festival 155
Seagram Building 56-
Sloppy Louie's 146
Staten Island Ferry 144
Statue of Liberty 1
Television Studios 30
Time & Life Building 24
Times Square 10
Trinity Church 135
United Nations 80
Upstairs at the Downstairs 76
U. S. Custom House 140
Verrazano-Narrows Bridge 176
Waldorf-Astoria Hotel 55
Wall Street 131
Washington Arch 36
Washington Mews 123
Wollman Memorial Rink 96
Woolworth Building 143
Yankee Stadium 108
Yorkville 105

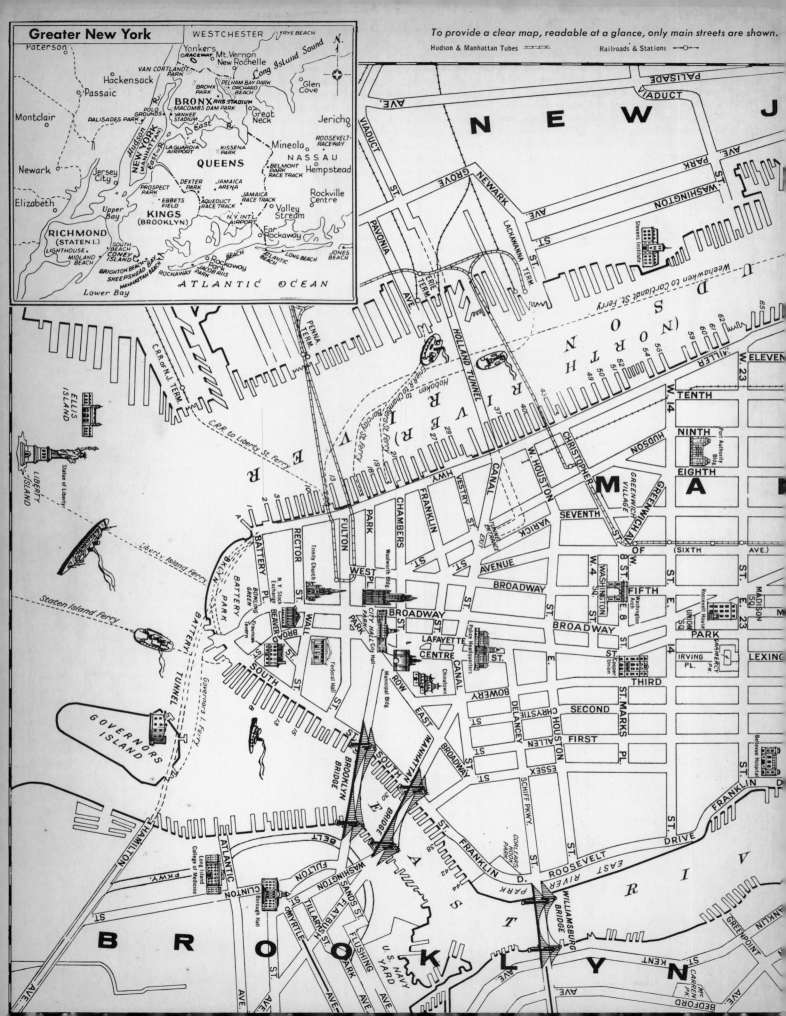